This symbol appears on some pages throughout this book. It indicates that adult supervision is advisable for that activity.

This edition published in 2004 by
Franklin Watts
96 Leonard Street
London
EC2A 4XD

Franklin Watts Australia
45-51 Huntley Street
Alexandria
NSW 2015

Cover design: Alice Young
Editor: Hazel Poole
Consultant: David Lambert
Designer: Sally Boothroyd
Photography: John Butcher
Artwork: Ruth Levy / Joanne Cowne
Models: Emma Morris
Picture Research: Ambreen Husain

ISBN 0 7496 5908 4

A CIP catalogue record is available for this book at the British Library.

ANIMALS

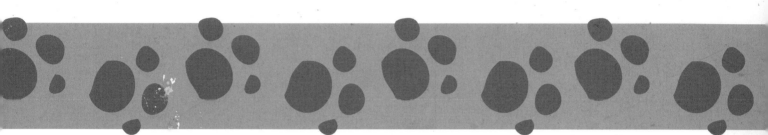

Ting and Neil Morris

Illustrated by Ruth Levy

W
FRANKLIN WATTS
LONDON·SYDNEY

Contents

Introduction

In this book you can learn about animals both by reading about them and by having fun with craft activities. The information in the fact boxes will tell you about animals from all over the world - where and how they live, and why many of them are endangered. As the world changes and human beings use up more of the earth's natural resources, so life becomes more difficult for many wild animals. If we learn more about them, perhaps we can help them to survive.

At the end of the book is a map to show you where some of the animals mentioned in the book live. There is also a list of places to visit if you want to find out more.

But now you can get your fingers sticky - making animals as you read about them.

Equipment and materials

The projects in this book provide an introduction to the use of different art and craft media, and need little adult help. Most of the objects are made with throwaway household "junk" such as boxes, plastic bottles and containers, newspaper and fabric remnants. Natural things such as seeds, sticks, sand and stones are also used. Paints, brushes, glues and modelling materials will have to be bought, but if stored correctly will last for a long time and for many more craft activities.

In this book, the following materials are used:

air-hardening clay
balloons (round)
beads
bowl (large)
brushes (for glue and paint)
bucket
buttons
cardboard tubes
chairs
comb (old)
cooking oil
cotton thread
craft knife
crayons
cup
egg-boxes
fabric scraps
felt pens
felt scraps
flour
foam chips
fork
funnel

garden wire
gloves, black and red
glue (water-based PVA, which can be used for thickening paint and as a varnish; strong glue such as UHU for sticking plastic, metal and fabric; glue stick)
jar (for mixing paint and paste)
knife
lolly stick
marker pen, black
newspaper
paint (powder, ready-mixed or poster paints)
paper (thick and thin card; corrugated paper; crêpe paper; tissue paper; tracing paper; newspaper; sugar paper; cartridge paper)
paper fasteners
pencils
plastic bottle

rolling-pin
ruler
salt
sand
scissors
silver foil
socks (old), white and brown
sponge
stapler
stocking
straws
string
tape (sticky tape; parcel tape)
toothpick
varnish (PVA mixed with cold water)
wallpaper paste (fungicide-free)
washing powder
washing-up liquid
water
wrapped sweets

Paper Tiger

Here's a fun way to make a tiger pencil-tidy or popcorn-holder.

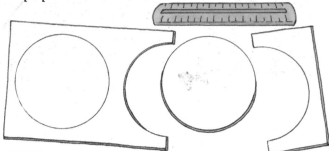

1 Start with the tiger's body, which is made from two containers. For the base of the containers, draw two circles about 8 cm in diameter onto some card. Cut out the two card discs.

2 Now cut two long strips of corrugated paper, about 26 cm long and 10 cm wide. The corrugated lines should run across the width of the strips. Paint the strips orange.

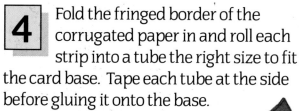

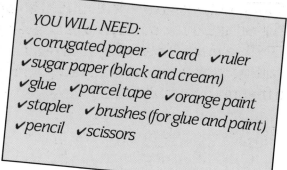

3 When the strips are dry, cut 1-cm slits into every second corrugated line.

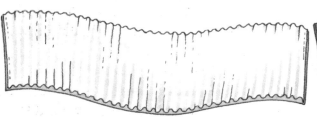

4 Fold the fringed border of the corrugated paper in and roll each strip into a tube the right size to fit the card base. Tape each tube at the side before gluing it onto the base.

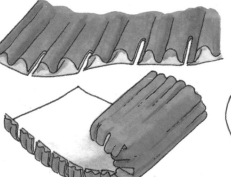

5 Staple the two tubes together as shown. To complete the tiger's body, cut some black strips of paper and stick them onto the tubes to look like stripes.

6 The tiger's head is made from a rectangular piece of card, with two card circles for eyes. Add two corrugated-paper ears and secure them with tape at the back. Paint the card orange to match the body.

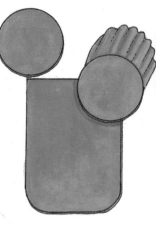

7 Cut out a pair of cream sugar-paper eyes and black pupils. Make a nose by folding a piece of black sugar paper in half and cutting it to shape. An orange card ring makes a friendly tiger smile.

8 Glue on the eyes and nose. Now tape the head to the body.

9 Help the tiger to sit comfortably by gluing on four corrugated-paper legs. Don't forget to staple on a long sugar-paper tail.

Now that your tiger is finished, why not fill him with popcorn and get munching?

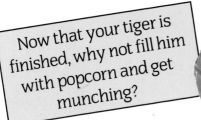

Tigers

Tigers are "big cats", a group of the cat family. Today they are mostly found in the jungles and forests of Asia. They are usually about 3 metres long, but the Siberian tiger (above) can reach 4 metres in length. It is the biggest of all cats, and its fur is long and thick which keeps it warm in the cold winters. The Indian, or Bengal, tiger lives in a much warmer southern climate and is smaller, with shorter, thinner fur.

Tigers usually hunt alone and at night, feeding on antelopes and other animals. They sometimes travel great distances to find food and water.

A tigress usually gives birth to two or three cubs. At the age of six or eight weeks, the cubs start to go hunting with their mother. They usually stay with her for at least a year, until they can hunt for themselves.

Today, tigers are in danger of dying out. Many have been killed for sport, although there are strict laws about hunting. Their natural homes are also being destroyed, along with their major food source of wild pigs, buffalo and deer.

Panda Puppets

YOU WILL NEED:
- ✔ 2 old socks, white and brown   ✔ scissors
- ✔ 2 gloves, black and red   ✔ strong glue
- ✔ black, white and brown felt   ✔ string
- ✔ material or tissue paper for stuffing
- ✔ black marker pen   ✔ 2 buttons

1 To make the giant panda's head, loosely stuff the foot of a white sock with material or tissue paper. Put on the black glove and push your gloved hand into the sock, so that your three big fingers can work the head. Tie some string around the neck, but leave it loose enough for your fingers to go in and out.

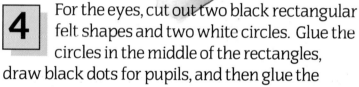

2 Cut two small holes in the sock below the neck. Pull the thumb and little finger of the glove through the holes to make the panda's arms.

3 Stick two black felt circles to the panda's head for the ears.

4 For the eyes, cut out two black rectangular felt shapes and two white circles. Glue the circles in the middle of the rectangles, draw black dots for pupils, and then glue the eyes into position.

Pandas

Giant pandas (left), with their black and white markings, are very rare. They live in the mountainous bamboo forests of western China, and are now protected by law in China. Giant pandas spend most of their time eating. In the summer they eat young bamboo shoots, and in the winter they feed on stalks and leaves. They grow up to 1.5 metres long and can sometimes weigh more than 150 kilograms.

The red, or lesser, panda (right) is smaller and lives in Western China and in the forests of the Himalayas. Red pandas feed on roots and insects as well as bamboo. They have reddish-brown fur and a long bushy tail and are related to the raccoons of North America.

5 Finally, stick on a black felt nose and a friendly mouth. Slip your gloved hand into the panda's head and make him nod to say hello.

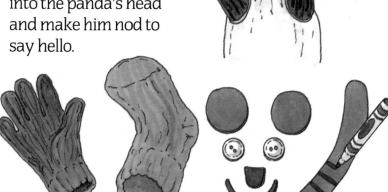

6 You could use the same method, with a brown sock and a red glove, to make a red panda. Add some brown felt ears and sew on two button eyes. To make the long striped tail, cut a strip of brown felt and mark it with black marker pen. Stick the tail to the brown sock body.

Now you can have fun with a different panda on each hand!

9

Penguin Bookend

1 Pour two cupfuls of sand or salt into an empty plastic bottle, using a funnel or paper cone. The sand or salt will keep the bookend from tipping over.

YOU WILL NEED:
✓ plastic bottle ✓ sand or salt ✓ newspaper
✓ wallpaper paste (fungicide-free) ✓ tape ✓ cup
✓ black poster paint ✓ white ready-mixed paint
✓ varnish ✓ brushes ✓ funnel ✓ thick card
✓ scissors ✓ yellow poster paint

2 Screw one sheet of newspaper into a ball and then wrap it in another sheet. Twist the four corners of the second sheet together, making a neat ball for the penguin's head.

3 Push the twisted end of the head into the bottle.

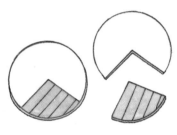

4 To make the beak, cut a circle, approximately 8 cm in diameter, from a piece of thick card. Cut a segment out of the circle as shown. Pull the edges together and fasten them. Tape the cone beak to the head.

5 Tear some newspaper into thin strips, about 2 cm wide. Mix the wallpaper paste as instructed on the packet and coat the strips of newspaper with it. Pull each strip between your finger and thumb to remove any lumps.

6 Paste four layers of newspaper strips over the head, beak and neck of the bottle. Leave to dry for a while. Add another three layers of coated newspaper strips. Leave to dry thoroughly, which might take a few days.

7 When the figure is dry, paint it with white ready mixed paint. Wait for this to dry and then paint the head black, leaving white circles for the eyes and adding black dots for the pupils. Paint the penguin's back black too, and add black flippers. For a shiny finish, varnish the whole model.

Penguins

Penguins are birds, but they cannot fly. Their wings are flippers, and they use them to swim at speeds of nearly 50 kilometres an hour. On land, penguins use their flippers for balancing as they walk. Sometimes they flop on their bellies and toboggan across ice and snow. Penguins spend most of their lives in the water. They come on land mainly to produce their young, living together in breeding grounds called rookeries. A rookery may contain as many as a million penguins! Many species, including the Adélie (above) and chinstrap penguins of the Antarctic, build nests of stones. The male and female take turns to sit on the nest and keep the eggs warm. While one is on the nest, the other goes to sea to feed on fish. Chicks leave the nest when they are about 4 weeks old. Sometimes harsh weather kills the eggs or chicks, but the parents usually manage to raise one chick to full growth.

When it's dry, you can put your penguin bookend to use. Have you got any books on the Antarctic to prop up?

Jumping Jack Monkey

1 Copy these monkey shapes onto thin card and cut them out. Remember to draw two arms and two legs, and turn one of each over before colouring them in.

2 Draw the monkey's face with felt pen. Colour in the body with crayon, making it look like fur.

3 Ask an adult to make ten holes in the pieces, as marked. Then fit your monkey together with paper fasteners. Don't make them too tight — make sure the arms and legs can move freely.

4 Join the arms and legs together at the back with string as shown. Then, with the arms and legs in the outstretched position, link the two strings with another piece of string, as shown. Leave a length of string hanging down at the front and tie a bead to the end.

New World monkeys

The New World monkeys of South and Central America are generally smaller than monkeys found in Asia and Africa. They live in trees and are mainly vegetarian. Most sleep at night and are active only in daylight. Marmosets and tamarins are small monkeys, which have claws instead of fingernails. Many have tufts of hair on their ears, face or neck. All other New World monkeys belong to one family, but they vary in appearance. Squirrel monkeys live in large troops and scamper about in the trees. Capuchins also live in the trees and use their long tails to grasp branches. Owl monkeys have big eyes and come out at night. Howlers are so called because the males have a very loud calling voice. Spider monkeys (above) are long-legged creatures that use their tail as a fifth hand.

5 Attach a string loop to the back of the head with parcel tape. Then you can hang him on your wall. Pull on the bead and watch the monkey jump!

The Great Kangaroo Race

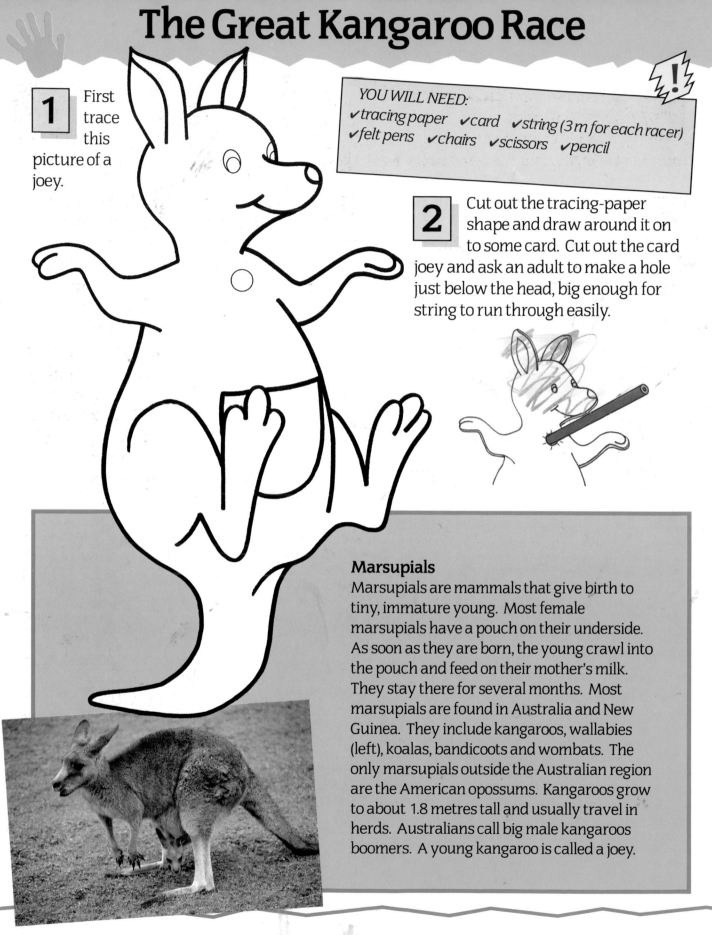

1 First trace this picture of a joey.

2 Cut out the tracing-paper shape and draw around it on to some card. Cut out the card joey and ask an adult to make a hole just below the head, big enough for string to run through easily.

Marsupials

Marsupials are mammals that give birth to tiny, immature young. Most female marsupials have a pouch on their underside. As soon as they are born, the young crawl into the pouch and feed on their mother's milk. They stay there for several months. Most marsupials are found in Australia and New Guinea. They include kangaroos, wallabies (left), koalas, bandicoots and wombats. The only marsupials outside the Australian region are the American opossums. Kangaroos grow to about 1.8 metres tall and usually travel in herds. Australians call big male kangaroos boomers. A young kangaroo is called a joey.

3 Make more identical kangaroo racers — as many as there are players. Colour them in and number their pouches 1, 2, 3 and so on.

4 Thread each kangaroo on to a length of string and tie one end to the leg of a chair. Lie the racers on their backs, with their racing numbers showing.

5 Mark a start line about 3 metres away from the chair, and a finish line near the chair.

6 Now each player takes a string and races their kangaroo by pulling on the string and then letting it go. Let each player practise a bit before starting. *(Here's a racing tip: don't jerk too hard or your racing joey will somersault backwards.)*

The first racer to cross the finish line wins the great kangaroo race!

Noah's Ark

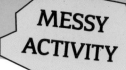

YOU WILL NEED:
- ✔ air-hardening clay
- ✔ toothpick
- ✔ poster paints
- ✔ card
- ✔ straws
- ✔ rolling-pin
- ✔ brushes
- ✔ water
- ✔ knife
- ✔ scissors
- ✔ small box
- ✔ poster paints

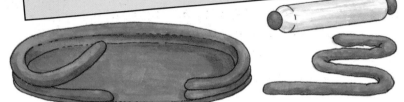

In the Bible story, Noah builds an ark because the earth is going to be flooded. The ark holds Noah's family and two of every sort of animal in the world. Our ark can't do that, but we are going to fill it with some of the biggest animals in the world — those of the African savannah.

1 To make the ark, flatten a ball of clay and roll it into an oval to form the bottom of the boat. Then roll some clay into a sausage shape as thick as your finger. Fit this coil carefully around the edge of the bottom of the ark. Now build up the sides of the ark with two more coils, one on top of the other, leaving a gap for the gangway plank. Moisten the edges and joints with water to help them stick.

2 For the cabin, roll out some clay and cover a small box. Then roll out some clay to make the gangway plank, and mark the "boards" with a toothpick. Now you need some animals to go up the gangway.

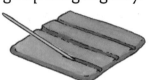

3 To make a tall giraffe, roll out a thick clay sausage for the body. Cut the ends, bend it and stand it up. Roll out a long, thin sausage, and shape one end to make the head. Mark the eyes with a toothpick. Put the two pieces together by moistening the joint. Add triangular ears and a tail.

4 Make a big elephant by rolling a lump of clay into a ball for the body. Make a smaller ball for the head and stick them together.

For the elephant's legs, cut a fat clay sausage into four equal parts and stick them beneath the body. Smooth the joints together.

A thin sausage makes the trunk and tail. Flatten two lumps of clay for the big ears and stick them to the head. Cut two tusks out of card and push them into the clay. Mark the eyes and trunk with a toothpick.

5 You can use the same method to make a rhino and a lion, stretching and pulling the clay ball into the animal shape. Press two card triangles into the clay for the rhino's horns. Use cut-up straws for the lion's mane.

Animals of the savannah

The savannah is an area of open grassland, scattered with bushes and flat-topped trees. In Africa, the savannah borders on tropical rainforests and deserts. These grasslands are the home of great herds of animals. The African elephant is the largest land animal, standing 3 to 4 metres high and weighing 3 to 6 tonnes. The leader of an elephant herd is usually an old female. The giraffe is the tallest animal, some standing more than 5.5 metres high. African rhinoceroses have huge, heavy bodies and two horns above their nostrils. They usually travel alone, but are sometimes found in small family groups. Zebras and antelopes live in herds and are hunted by lions. The "king of beasts" lives in prides of between 10 and 35 lions.

6 Finally, make a zebra. Roll out two sausages for the legs. Then roll a thicker piece for the body. Join them together in a letter "H" shape, smooth the joints and bend the legs down.

Add a piece of clay for the head and neck, and don't forget to give your zebra ears and a tail.

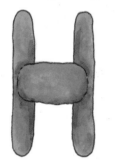

7 When the animals are dry, paint them before putting them into the ark.

Why not make more birds and animals to go into your ark?

17

Tortoise Surprise

Tortoises are very slow animals, and this one takes quite a long time to make!

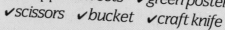

YOU WILL NEED:
- ✔ round balloon ✔ 3 toilet-roll tubes ✔ newspaper ✔ tissue paper
- ✔ wallpaper paste (fungicide-free) ✔ buttons ✔ PVA glue ✔ brush
- ✔ wrapped sweets ✔ green poster paint ✔ string ✔ warm water
- ✔ scissors ✔ bucket ✔ craft knife

1 First tear up some newspaper into lots of 2-cm squares. To make paper pulp, fill a bucket with paper pieces. Pour some warm water into the bucket and leave the paper to soak. When the paper is soft, rub it into a pulp. Then squeeze out the water. Mix the wallpaper paste as instructed on the packet, and then stir it into the pulp until the mixture is like sticky pastry. *(Keep any unused paste in a separate container.)*

2 For the tortoise's body, blow up a balloon. Cover it with the pulp and press some dry newspaper pieces into the paste. Smooth out any air bubbles, and cover the balloon with three layers of pulp and paper.

3 Cut two toilet-roll tubes for legs as shown, and cover each leg with a layer of pulp and newspaper pieces.

4 Stick the curved edge of the legs to the body, using pasted strips to hold them in position.

5 Use another toilet-roll tube to make the neck. For the head, make a paper ball and stick it into the open end of the neck. Stick it to the body with pasted strips.

6 Now cover the head, neck, legs, top and sides of the tortoise's body with paper pulp and smooth the pulp with your hands. Don't cover the underside. Then leave the tortoise to dry, which might take a few days.

7 When your tortoise is dry, ask an adult to cut an opening in the underside. Then fill it with sweets and cover the opening with tissue paper.

8 To hang the tortoise up, make a small hole in the top of the body. Push the knotted end of a piece of string into the hole and put PVA glue and pulp around the hole. Let this dry.

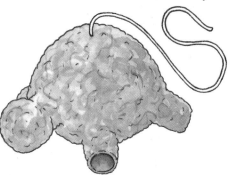

9 Paint the tortoise with green poster paint and glue on pieces of coloured tissue paper to make a shell. Stick on some button eyes.

You can play a good party game with your tortoise by hanging it up and using it as a Mexican piñata. Blindfold one of your friends, give them a rolled-up newspaper to use as a stick, and then spin them around. If she or he manages to hit the tortoise, they may have a sweet surprise!

Turtles and tortoises

Sea turtles are water reptiles with paddle-like flippers and a streamlined shell. They can be found in most seas and often travel long distances to lay eggs on their favourite nesting beaches. It is thought that the first turtles lived on earth more than 185 million years ago and that they have changed very little since then.

The largest turtle is the leatherback, which is found worldwide. It can be over 2 metres long and weigh over 500 kilograms. The leatherback has a thick, leathery skin covering its shell. Turtles are graceful and swift swimmers, but clumsy and slow on land.

Land-dwellers are usually called tortoises. A rare type of giant tortoise (below) lives only on the Galapagos Islands in the Pacific Ocean. It can grow up to 1.3 metres long and has a big high-domed shell. It moves very slowly on its tough scaly legs.

Rainforest Screen

1 Cut off the top, the bottom and one side of a large cardboard box, leaving just three sides. These will form your screen. Stand it up to see how it looks.

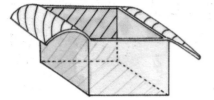

YOU WILL NEED:
- large cardboard box
- green powder paint
- yellow, green and brown ready-mixed paint
- crayons ✔ PVA glue
- strong glue ✔ sugar paper
- tissue paper ✔ silver foil
- corrugated paper ✔ tape
- crêpe paper ✔ felt scraps
- old stocking ✔ scissors
- foam chips or fabric stuffing
- fine sand or salt ✔ card
- brushes (for glue and paint)

2 Lie the screen flat while you are working on your picture. You can mark the position of trees and animals with crayon. Cut out some tall corrugated-paper tree trunks. Paint them different shades of green and brown and stick them onto the screen. Stick crêpe- or tissue-paper vegetation on top.

3 Make lianas (climbing plants) from strips of twisted crêpe paper, and wind them around the tree trunks. Cut leaf shapes from paper and tape only the stems to the tree, to produce a three-dimensional effect.

4 Cut out some colourful sugar-paper petals and stick them to the trees. Make clusters of fruit with crumpled-up tissue paper.

5 Use crunched-up silver foil for a rainforest river. Stick the foil to the bottom of the screen and cover the forest floor with green vegetation. To make the vegetation, mix fine sand or salt with dry green powder paint. Brush glue between the plants and the river. Then sprinkle the coloured sand over the glue while it is still wet. Pick the screen up and shake off the loose sand.

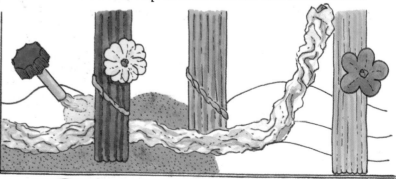

6 For the bird's body, cut a card circle, approximately 5cm in diameter. Fold it in half.

For the head, draw two small circles, cut them out and stick them onto each side of the body and join them together. Add some eyes.

Fold a piece of coloured paper as shown to make the tail. Stick it into the body and cut the end at an angle.

To make the beak, fold a rectactangular piece of card in half and cut away the shaded areas shown here. Make a small cut in the fold and slot the beak onto the bird's head.

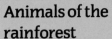

Animals of the rainforest

Many different types of animals live in tropical rainforests. In South American forests, howler and spider monkeys swing from the branches. The howler's booming call might be accompanied by the harsh cries of a blue and gold macaw, a large tropical parrot with a long tail and brilliant plumage. The toucan, with its huge, brightly-coloured bill, also lives here. Lower down, there are rainforest reptiles. The emerald tree boa (above) winds its body around branches. This snake has very long teeth which help it to catch and hold birds. Many insects make their home here too. The hercules beetle has two large curved horns, and the huge Morpho butterfly has beautiful, bright blue wings. Jaguars live deep in the forest. All these animals form part of the balance of nature which will sadly be lost if the rainforests continue to be destroyed.

7 For a slithering snake, stuff a stocking with fabric or foam and knot the end. Make eyes and a mouth out of felt scraps. Add the snake's markings with paint thickened with PVA glue. Wrap the snake around the top or side of the screen.

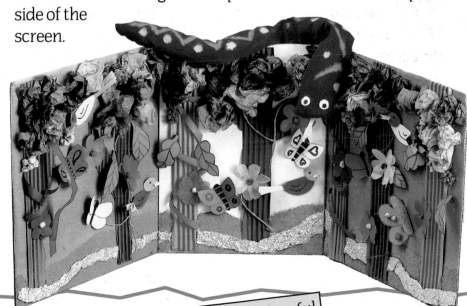

Why not add some colourful card butterflies?

Sea World

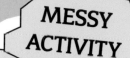
1 To turn your box into a tropical sea world, cut it as shown here.

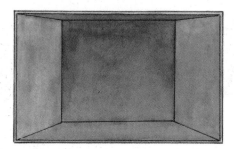

YOU WILL NEED:
- large shallow cardboard box   ✔ scissors
- ✔ sugar paper   ✔ large sheet of white paper
- ✔ felt pens   ✔ tape   ✔ PVA glue   ✔ glue stick
- ✔ pink tissue paper   ✔ washing powder
- ✔ green, blue and yellow powder paint   ✔ water
- ✔ washing-up liquid   ✔ cotton thread   ✔ sponge
- ✔ comb (old)   ✔ brushes (for glue and paint)

2 Mix together three tablespoons of washing powder with six spoonfuls of blue powder paint. Add some water until the mixture is thick and creamy. Make up the same amount of green paint. Paint the inside of the box with layers of blue and green. Make gently swirling currents with your fingers.

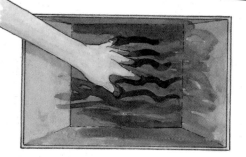

3 While the sea background is drying, you can start on the underwater vegetation. Mix up some yellow, blue and green powder paint by mixing each colour with washing-up liquid and a little water. Sponge the yellow paint onto a sheet of paper, adding green and blue blobs. Make twirling patterns with a comb.

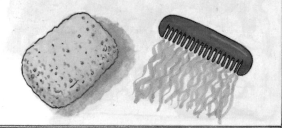

4 When the painted paper is dry, add some wavy sea plants with felt pen. Leaving a fold along the bottom edge of the paper, cut around the plants. Stick the fold to the bottom of your box. For bits of coral reef, crumple up pink tissue paper and glue different-shaped clusters to the bottom.

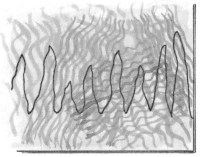

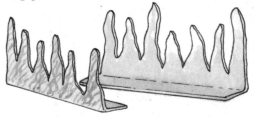

5 Cut lots of fish, big and small, from sugar paper. Colour them brightly with crayons and felt pens.

6 Cut different lengths of cotton thread and stick them to the fish.

Tape the threads to the top of the box and take a dive into your own sea world.

Why not add a floating jellyfish as well?

The Great Barrier Reef

This is the largest group of coral reefs in the world, stretching for 2,000 kilometres along the coast of Queensland, Australia. It is separated from the mainland by shallow water. Coral reefs are built up by millions of tiny sea animals called coral polyps. Along with algae, these deposit limestone, and bind together to form a reef. Over millions of years, the reef has become many metres thick, with an outer layer of living coral. The Great Barrier Reef is the world's largest marine park. Almost 1,500 different species of fish live in its waters. Brightly coloured angelfish, butterfly fish, spiny-finned surgeonfish and manta rays all live and breed there. The warm waters are also home to 4,000 species of shellfish, as well as sea turtles. The entire reef area is protected, and it is illegal for divers to break off or take away coral.

Card Crocodile

1 With a large supply of card and crêpe paper you can create an enormous crocodile. Use four large pieces of card of equal width and varying lengths to make tubes of different sizes. Tape each tube as shown so that one opening is a bit smaller than the other.

2 The smallest piece of card should form a cone shape for the tail.

3 Fit the four tubes into a rocket shape and tape them together. Now you have made the crocodile's body.

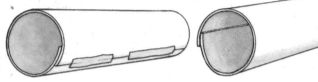

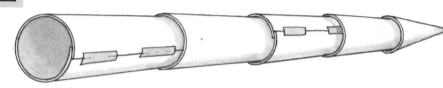

4 Use three flat egg-box tops for the top jaw and three for the bottom jaw. Tape the cartons together.

5 Attach the jaws to the body.

6 Cut strips of crêpe paper approximately 10 cm wide. Wet them with diluted PVA glue and wrap them around the whole body and jaws.

7 Use toilet-roll tubes covered with crêpe paper to make four legs. Stick clawlike feet, made from black card, to the bottom of each leg. Attach the legs to the body with sticky tape. Wrap crêpe paper strips around the joins.

8 Line the inside of the croc's mouth with pink sugar paper, cut to shape.

Crocodiles and alligators

Crocodiles and alligators are large reptiles belonging to a group called the crocodilians. They all have large powerful jaws and long tails, and their skin is like hard leather. They spend their lives in or close to water, mostly in freshwater lakes, rivers or swamps, but sometimes in coastal waters. They swim with twisting strokes of their tail, holding their short legs close to their body. Crocodiles have long, pointed snouts and live in parts of North and South America, Australia, Africa and Asia. Large crocodiles grow up to 6 metres in length. Alligators (above) have a broad, rounded snout and live in China and in the Americas, including southern Florida, USA. Crocodilians lay eggs and some mothers carry the young in their mouths to the water's edge. They stay there for several months, learning to swim and catch food. Crocodilians feed on fish, birds and almost any other animal they can catch!

9 Cut strips of jagged teeth from white card. Glue them to the jaws.

Add two red card circles for his nostrils, and two big yellow card eyes. Draw the pupils with black felt pen

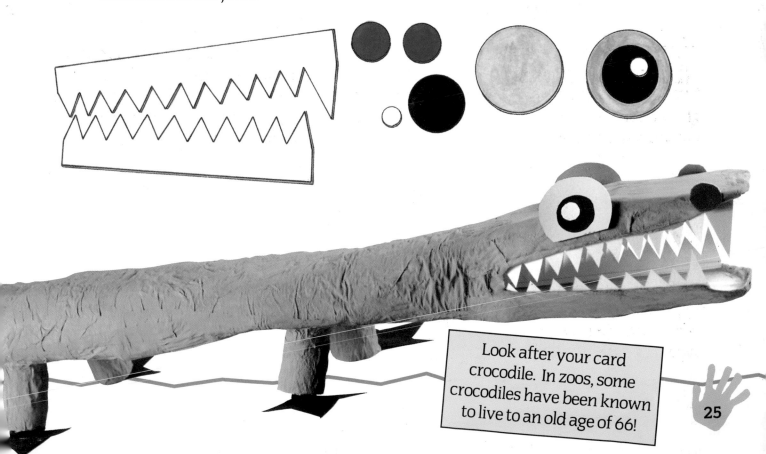

Look after your card crocodile. In zoos, some crocodiles have been known to live to an old age of 66!

Termitarium

Worker termites build their termitarium with particles of soil. You can make a model of a termites' nest with lumps of dough.

 YOU WILL NEED:
- shoebox lid or other cardboard base
- 6 cups of flour ✔ 3 cups of salt
- 3 tablespoons of cooking oil ✔ fork
- water ✔ gardening wire ✔ large bowl
- white and brown ready-mixed paint
- brushes ✔ lolly stick

1 Mix the flour and salt in a large bowl. Add the cooking oil and enough water to make a pliable mixture. Knead and squeeze the mixture until it feels like clay. If it is too dry, add more water. If it is too wet, add more flour.

2 Put a large lump of clay in the middle of the shoebox lid, and pat it into a wide base. Now you can build the ground floor of the termitarium. Roll out a long dough sausage and use it to build a maze of narrow passages. Shape small rooms with lumps of dough and make a big room for the queen. In real life, the whole nest is full of passages, right up to the top!

3 Now you can cover the inside of the nest. Place most of the dough on top of it, and form it into a high structure. Make a mountain with crags and peaks. Use a lolly stick or fork to give a rugged texture, copying the photograph of a real nest. Then paint the termitarium brown.

4 You could make some workers, the termites that build the nest, with any left-over dough. Roll a round head in the palm of your hand. Then make a pear-shaped body and mark segments with a lolly stick.

5 Stick the head and body together with water. Ask an adult to cut some short lengths of gardening wire for legs and feelers. Bend the six legs and two feelers into position and stick them into the dough. Make lots of worker termites.

6 Paint the termites white and arrange them around the termitarium.

Termites

Termites are sometimes called white ants, but they are actually related to cockroaches and grasshoppers and can usually be found in warm countries. They live in colonies in three separate groups. The first is the royal group. Each colony has a king and queen - fully developed winged termites whose job is to reproduce. It is thought that kings and queens sometimes live for up to 50 years. The second group is made up of workers who are small, blind and wingless. They make the nest, or termitarium, and collect food for the colony. The third group, the soldiers, have hard heads and strong jaws. They defend the colony against attack, mainly from ants.

Some termites build huge mounds from bits of soil mixed with saliva. These nests contain a maze of narrow passages with small rooms to store food and eggs. There is a large room for the queen. The mounds can be six metres high and five metres across at the base.

Animals Around the World

 Giraffe

 Koala

 Penguin

 Crocodile

 Turtle

 Elephant

 Rhinoceros

 Lion

 Panda

 Indian Tiger

 Angelfish

 Kangaroo

North America

Central America

South America

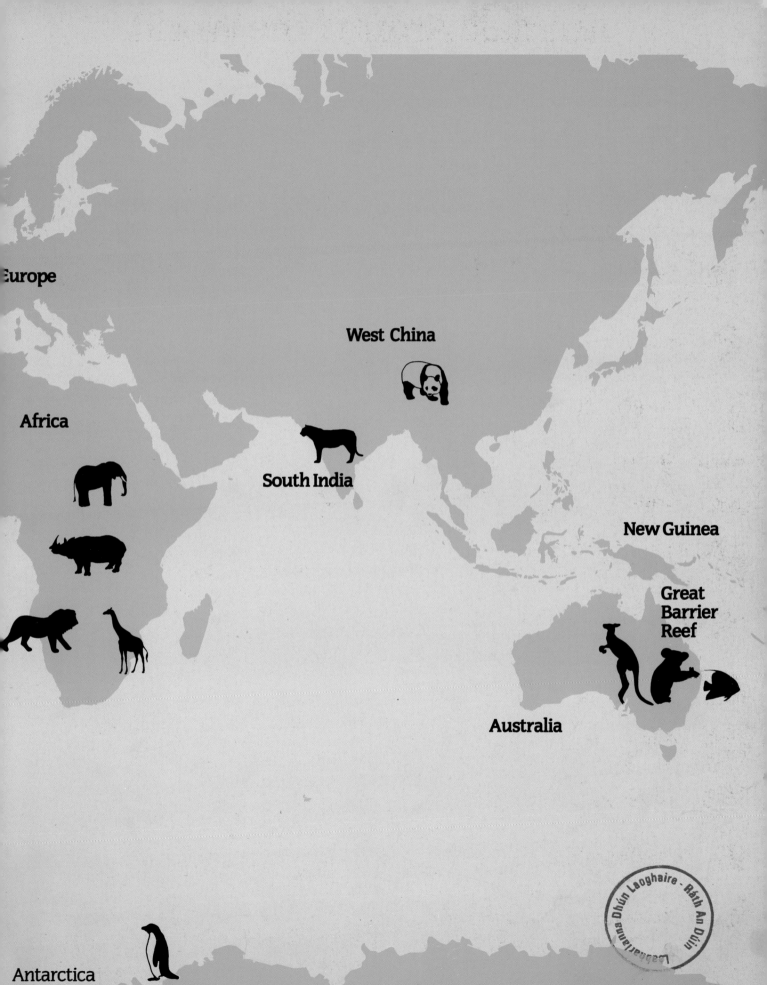

Europe

West China

Africa

South India

New Guinea

Great
Barrier
Reef

Australia

Antarctica

Glossary

Amazonian forest - the tropical rainforest around the River Amazon in Brazil, South America; the biggest rainforest in the world.

ark - the boat that Noah built.

bamboo - a tall treelike grass, one of the world's fastest growing plants.

colony - a large group of animals living together.

continent - one of the Earth's large land masses.

coral - tiny sea animals and plants bound together, forming a reef.

crocodilians - crocodiles and alligators.

cub - a young tiger, lion, bear, etc.

Himalayas - mountain range in South Asia, between China and Nepal, - the highest in the world.

joey - a young kangaroo

litter - a group of baby animals produced at one birth.

mammal - a warm-blooded backboned animal whose young feed on their mother's milk.

marsupial - a pouched mammal.

New World monkeys - a family of different monkeys living in Central and South America; the New World is another name for the Americas.

pride - a group of lions.

rainforest - thick forest found in tropical areas of heavy rainfall.

reptile - a cold-blooded backboned animal, such as a snake or a crocodile.

rookery - penguins' breeding ground.

saliva - fluid in the mouth that prepares food for swallowing.

savannah - open grassland scattered with bushes and trees in tropical Africa.

snout - the nose and jaws of a crocodilian or other animal

species - a group of related animals or plants; for example, lions and tigers are different species of the cat family.

termitarium - the nest of a termite colony.

tropical - situated in the tropics, the hottest part of the Earth's surface near the equator.

vegetarian - an animal which eats only plants, not meat.

Useful Websites

www.kidsdomain.com/craft/ provides step-by-step instructions and photographs for a range of themed craft activities.

www.crafts4kids.com includes a variety of craft projects from around the world. Step-by-step instructions are given, as well as printable templates.

www.dltk-kids.com/animals has a fun selection of craft projects based on a range of animals, including Australian animals, farm animals and animals from the rainforest.

Places to visit
United Kingdom

Glasgow Zoopark
Calderpark, Uddingston
Glasgow G71 7RZ
www.glasgowzoo.co.uk

London Zoo
Regents Park
London NW1 4RY
www.londonzoo.co.uk

National Wetlands Centre Wales
Penclacwydd
Llwynhendy
Llanelli SA14 9SH
www.wwt.org.uk

London Wetland Centre
Queen Elizabeth's Walk
Barnes
London SW13 9WT
www.wwt.org.uk

Woburn Safari Park
Woburn Park
Bedfordshire MK17 9QN
www.woburnsafari.co.uk

Australia

Australia Zoo
Glass House Mountains
Tourist Route, Beerwah
Queensland 4519
www.crocodilehunter.com

Victoria's Open Range Zoo, Werribee
'K' Road, Werribee
Vic 3030
www.zoo.org.au

Caversham Wildlife Park
Lord Street, Whiteman
Western Australia 6028
www.cavershamwildlife.com.au

Note to parents and teachers
Every effort has been made by the Publishers to ensure that these websites are suitable for children; that they are of the highest educational value, and that they contain no inappropriate or offensive material. However, because of the nature of the Internet, it is impossible to guarantee that the contents of these sites will not be altered. We strongly advise that Internet access is supervised by a responsible adult.

Index